It's Not Easy Being ORANGE

Dr. Skippy McNibbles

Design by Deborah Perdue,

Illumination Graphics

First Edition

Printed in U.S.A.

ISBN 978-0-578-57828-6

Dedication

Oh Dearest Dear Leader,
This book is for you,
It's not for Thing 1
No . . . Not for Thing 2
A cat in a hat
Or a mouse in a house
the Grinch, or a Who
or Samuel B Louse.
I wrote it for you!
you inspire me so
you can read it at STOP!
you can read it at GO!
You can read it aloud,
you can read it in bed,
you can read it alone,
you can read it with Ned.

Please oh Dear Leader
I hope that you see
This book that I wrote
in the land of the free
I'm sending it off though
To get printed by Xi . . .

Brown, black and yellow are allright to be.

But just try to be orange,

and then you will see,

The folks who all say that color is great

All laugh and point

And like to berate!

Why oh why

are others so cruel?

Life is unfair when you are a tool.

You'd think that my money would help

people tell,

That I'm smart and I'm funny and sexy

as hell.

Bein' orange ain't easy,

    not like being green

That silly ol frog is Mujahideen!

You can't believe a word from the runt

    He's Hillary's frog!

It's a total witch hunt!

#MeToo!

Oh nobody like me,

Nobody cares

Not even the woman

who styles my hair.

Gave her pussy a tickle

With a wink and a grin

She shouted #MeToo!

. . . it's that orange thing again. . .

I just don't get it

I'm a super great guy

If you look past my color

You'd finally see why

Orange makes me feel pretty!

It's not ugly like grey

So stop talking and listen

And do what I say!

Orange folks are just smarter!

And better in bed!

We're taller and thinner

And very well read.

We're leaders of men,

What more can I say?

Being orange is just better

Now get out of my way!

I'll show you all

What it's like to be great

I'm running for Pres

On a platform of hate!

You all are too happy!

There's so much to fear!

Like a caravan of Mexicans

And they're all coming here!

Black folks in cities

Are running amok!

Libtards are coming

For your gun and your truck!

Science is fake, the climate is fine!

It matters not though. . .

I'm going to get mine

My gut is much smarter

than most people's brains,

I know the real truth about hurricanes.

The Chinese are stealing all of our tech!

The real threat though, is up by Quebec...

They burned down the white house!

They drank all our beer!

They don't even care

If you claim to be queer!

It's certainly a crime in this day and age

That a smart guy like me has to pay

to get laid . . .

So I have a plan, just listen to me!

(Newspapers all lie I don't really like pee)

I got a call from this Vladamir guy,

He's coming to help!

And he'd never lie. . .

He knows some guys who can help hack the vote!

And said all I need, is a sleazy turncoat

So I'll send my boy

To hear the man out

If I don't get his help

I'll lose in a rout!

We need to control

   The message they hear

So I'll twitter and tweet

   Like William Shakespeare

The American Press

   Is our true enemy

So we'll lie and we'll cheat

   And we won't let them see

All the things that we do

To our citizenry

If the people don't like it,

If they shout and they yell,

I'll get all the pastors

To send em to hell!

I'll levy tariffs, and build a tall wall,

Where Humpty the liberal

Will hopefully fall.

If his balance is good just go push him down,

I'll pay your court costs,

And a night on the town!

So everyone vote, but just vote for me.

You know you can't trust crooked liar Hillary.

She's a nasty ol woman, you can tell by the smell.

We'll go lock her up

In a federal jail cell.

We'll protect all the statues

    of old racist pigs,

Burn all the coal.

    Trade deals? Renege.

We'll turn on our friends

  And trust enemies

Replace all respect

  With douchebaggery

Even when it's clear that I'm wrong,

I'll call it fake news

and keep plowing along.

I know in my heart that I'm always right.

Just go ask my mommy

I was tested! I'm bright!

We'll teargas and shoot

The little children

Don't lead em so much!

We can't let em in!

Oh God bless America!

The land of the free!

All those who died, for you and for me

Oh it's raining?

I see . . .

All this fake news is drowning me out!

They won't say what I want,

So I'll start a tryout.

For a new news network I'm going to sell.

I hope it does better

Than my casinos or XFL

Once I am in you can't make me leave.

I'm pres and you're not!

You're all so naïve.

But if people go, and vote me out;

I'll break all my toys!

I'll scream and shout!

It's gotta be fraud

Illegals are voting!

The blue wave is coming!

The press is misquoting!

So everyone get out.

Vote Y chromosome.

If you don't - screw you guys

I'm going home.

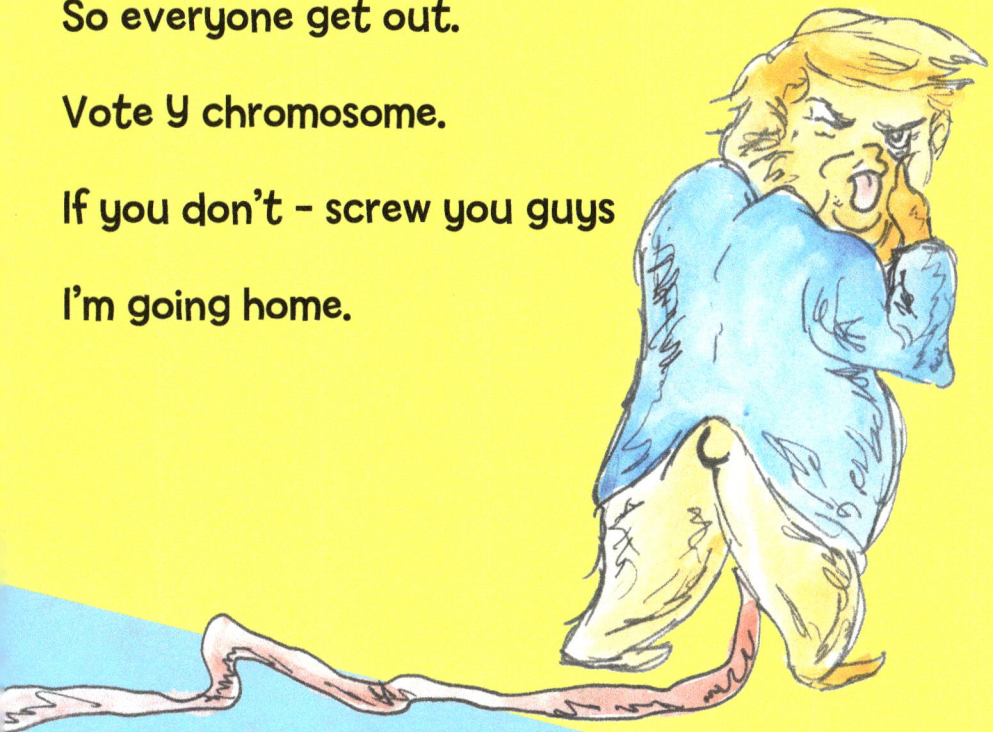